RENZO CHIARELLI

THE
GALLERY OF THE ACADEMY
AND THE
MUSEUM OF ST. MARK

TRANSLATED BY
SUSAN GLASSPOOL

BONECHI EDITORE FLORENCE

5, VIA DEI RUSTICI

Alla memoria di Luisa Marcucci

The GALLERY OF THE ACADEMY and the MUSEUM OF ST. MARK, because of their closeness and anyway consolidated tradition, form almost a unique museographic group, and are in fact considered as such by visitors and organised tourism.

The visit to the two Institutions can also be kept complementary to the ends of a unique and useful knowledge of a vast figurative cycle which is completed by the incomparable group of Michelangeloesque sculptures collected in an arc which starting from the first Florentine activity (the David) arrives at the full maturity of the artist.

Because of this fact, the Editor has thought of collecting and presenting a unique and selected visual synthesis of the principal works of the Academy and St. Mark.

THE GALLERY OF THE ACCADEMY

Among the Lorrain princes who governed in Tuscany for about a century, the most enlightened was the Grand Duke Pietro Leopoldo, who in 1784 decreed that all the schools and academies of drawing in existence in Florence were to be joined together in a single Academy, and he wished to build next to the school, a Gallery of the old masters in order to make it easier for the young students to study them. By this magnificent decision in 1784 the Gallery of the Academy was created and even today holds a position of importance second to none among the Florentine galleries. The Gallery was placed in the place in which we still find it today; the ancient and noble building was at one time a part of the Hospital of St. Matthew to which have been extended by many additional rooms (the last extension was in 1855) running from here, the one time convent of St. Nicolas, and joined with some already built as part of the Hard Stone Works.

The consistency and quality of the Academy collection has undergone considerable variations quite natural in the course of two centuries circa; for instance, the continuing additions to the original nucleus (in fact many art works of the Florentine churches and abolished convents are now here) and the frequent exchanges which have come about with other Florentine galleries and viceversa. Since, besides the old masters there were also exhibited works by modern artists, the Academy was the first home of the Gallery of Modern Art, which after the first world war was moved to the Pitti Palace. One can also say that for a long time the Gallery of the Academy was used as a depot for the more precious art works from the Uffizi until when in more recent times it was decided to have a more definite and permanent arrangement, partly carried out and partly still in plan form, with relative and progressive reorganisation of the rooms and preparation of the drawings of the graphic museum.

A crucial moment in the Academy's history was marked by the transfer there in 1873 of Michelangelo's David: the architect De Fabris designed a place in 1882 for the colossal statue, the so-called « Tribune », so as to look after it as it deserved. In the first years of the XIX century, other sculptures by Michelangelo were collected and arranged around David. Firstly the St. Matthew and the four Prisoners, to which were added the two original plaster casts by Giambologna, the Rape of the Sabine Women and the Virtue overwhelming Vice in 1911, and finally, in 1939, the Pietà of Palestrina. This group is particularly unique and great of Michelangelo's sculpture and forms the most illustrious and most fundamental nucleus of the collection of Academy: thanks to this group, the Florentine Gallery is able to compete in importance with the most celebrated Italian and foreign museums.

The Academy Gallery is actually on the ground floor of the building in Via Ricasoli — other than that there is a large hall with the Tribune of David — a series of other rooms of different dimensions of which three (the so-called « Byzantine » rooms) have a collection of paintings on wood, mostly of the Florentine school of the XII and XIV centuries; a larger room with three smaller ones (the « Florentine » rooms) are dedicated to a considerable collection of Tuscan paintings from the XV century; finally the last room (« Colossus ») is hung with famous paintings from the XVI century. On the walls of the Tribune are exhibited splendid tapestries of Florentine and Flemish manufacture of the XVI, XVII and XVIII centuries.

THE SCULPTURE OF
MICHELANGELO BUONARROTI

(Born in Caprese on March 6th 1475,
died in Rome on February 18th 1564)

THE SCULPTURE OF
MICHELANGELO BUONARROTI

(Born in Caprese on March 6th 1475,
died in Rome on February 18th 1564)

1

In 1501 the Cathedral Art Works Committee commissioned Michelangelo (the contract was signed on the 16th August) to carry out a statue of *David* which the artist had to carve out of an already badly dug into block of marble. This had been done in 1464 by Agostino di Duccio for a statue, which was never completed, to be placed outside Santa Maria del Fiore. The young Michelangelo worked on this, his first huge undertaking from when he was 26 until he was 29 years old, finishing in the April of 1504; in the September, by a decision made by a commission composed of the most famous Florentine artists, the statue was placed in front of the Signoria Palace, almost as a symbol and a defence of the reconquered Republican liberties. During a riot in 1527, the left arm of *David* was broken by a stone, and the fragments rescued by Salviati and Vasari; Cosimo I had the statue restored in 1543. In 1873 the David was taken away and placed in the Academy Gallery so as to preserve it better, and replaced on its old stand by a copy.

The impressive form of the sculpture (it is 4,10 metres high), the dynamic tension all over it, the bold and beautiful face, gazing with security at his adversary, the powerful and proud head, the very strong forceful lines of the anatomy and the muscles ready to spring, these things make clear the supreme dignity, moral and humane of the personage — from this moment of his youth — the superb vision of Michelangelo, who here entwines the Biblical champion in a heroic atmosphere. It is very different from the way in which David was depicted as humanely smiling by Donatello a little more than seventy years before. For Tolnay the *David* represents « the synthesis of the ideals of the Florentine Renaissance ».

The uneasy sense created by the « unfinished » works of Michelangelo is relieved at the Academy by another work of his youth, the St. Matthew, which should have formed part of a series of twelve statues of the Apostles, a commission by the Wool Guild to Michelangelo for Santa Maria del Fiore on the 24th April 1503 (the contract was cancelled in December 1505). Of the twelve statues, this was the only one to be roughed out by the sculptor before his departure in 1505 for Rome (some scholars consider nevertheless that this was the statue on which Michelangelo was still working in 1506). It stayed in the Works of the Cathedral until 1831 and was then taken to the Academy of Fine Art and from there in 1909 to the Gallery.

Some of the famous verses which Michelangelo has handed down to us, help us to understand this powerful figure of the Apostle which slowly and almost magically emerges from an indistinct and shapeless block, and these verses show so well in these and other works of the great artist, that the sculptor already sees the figure inside the marble that he has to draw out, freeing the lifeless material which held and contained it:

> « *The best artist has no concept*
> *To circumscribe only the marble itself*
> *Eliminiating the excess, and arrives at that only*
> *The hand which obeys the intellect* ».

In this case the force of the figure is so great and so dramatic the turning and twisting of the expressive parts or also only hints of the chisel to make it seem that the artist had deliberately left the sculpture (and it is this that is one of the fundamental data of the many vast problems of Michelangelo) beyond contingent events to a state of indeterminate form, however, what is more apparent than substantial, than difficult, to be able to think of an equally valid « completed work » of expression and arrival of different meanings.

One can say the same for the four statues of the Prisoners, which, together with *St. Matthew* make the most fascinating and extraordinary « gallery of statues » that it is possible to imagine. These « roughs » of the Prisoners (or Slaves), were given by the nephew of Michelangelo, Lionardo Buonarroti, to Cosimo I de' Medici who in his turn placed them in the grotto of Buontalenti in the Boboli Gardens, from where in 1909 they were transferred to the Academy Gallery.

Michelangelo had sculpted them for the tomb of Pope Julius II in St. Peters; (according to many scholars in around 1519 though others instead think much later, after 1532) the tomb never finished in the place designed for it and neither for the plan previous to that. Two other *Slaves*, today in the Louvre Museum, were also supposed to go on the tomb; these had huge proportions and were considered for the tomb as ornamental sculpture, worthy to provide the idea of the exceptional greatness of the design. The four *Prisoners* of the Academy, which, acording to Vasari, are an example of how one should « carve out the figures in marble with a chisel », are among the strongest and most terrifying testimonies of the great art of Michelangelo and of the

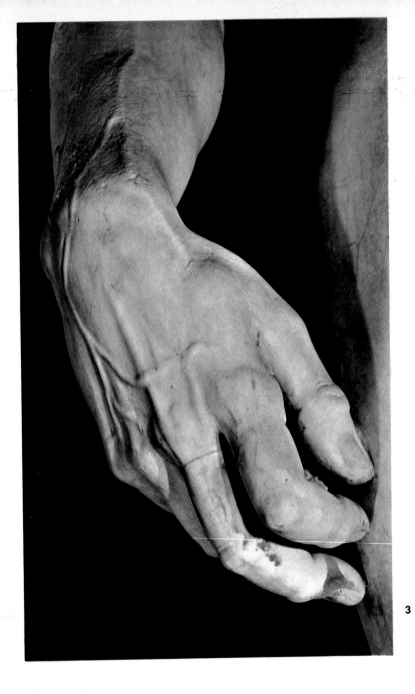

3   **4**

violent way, almost with fury in which the artist has attacked the marble; almost as though in effect he wished to free the Prisoners from the ugly material in which they were imprisoned. A titanic fight of the spirit and the intelligence against the adverse forces of life and nature. A fight most times to end in failure, the heroic rebellion of man unable to accept an adverse and cruel destiny; this is expressed by the *Prisoners* in their desperate wish for freedom, in the spasmodic tension of the Herculean muscles and on the rough and tortured surface over which the light flows inquiet and contrasting and without finding respite or pause. The supreme example is the disturbing statue of the *Prisoner* called « Atlas », who is fixed for eternity in the terrible and useless effort to free the head (from which we unconsciously feel the

invisible presence) from cyclopian mass which encloses him.

Last among the exceptional collection of sculptures is the *Pietà of Palestrina*, so, called because it was originally situated in the Chapel of the Barbarini Palace at Palestrina near Rome. Even now there is some passionate discussion among experts over this work. As it was never mentioned in the fountains, of history as a work of the Master, many critics dispute its authenticity (the first to use the name of

Michelangelo was Cecconi in 1756). Toesca was the first to support Michelangelo as being its author, followed by Venturi and other writers of history of art, but the scholars who disagree with them are equally numerous. Accordingly Tolnay eliminated the traditional attribution of the work to G. Lorenzo Bernini and says that the Pietà would be a result of « meditation » by a student on a theme of Michelangelo. The character of the group, so powerfully dramatic is nevertheless close to Michelangelo's later style of work.

7

8

1. - MASTER OF THE MAGDA-LEN (XIII cent.)
Mary Magdalen and the history of her Life (panel)

The personality of this anonimous painter of the XIII century, was reconstructed by Sirèn, based on the painting today at the Academy, with the portrait of Mary Magdalen in penitent's clothes flanked by eight stories of her life. This reconstruction by Sirèn is accepted by all critics; meanwhile the history of the painting is all the more discussed and one must consider it as belonging to the most advanced stage in the life of the unknown master: he was a Florentine artist with « Byzantine inspiration and influences from Pisa and Lucca », and putting all together has the form and the current composition of the late 13th century. As for Marcucci, who considers the painting abong the less important of the many attributed to the « Master of the Magdalen », the element most positive in the picture is a « somewhat popular immediateness in the telling of the little story, palidly resounding with purely romanic tradition ». However the lengthened and outlined figure of the Saint is not devoid of suggestion, and shows an intense spiritual concentration and covered in the long flowing hair which clothes her. At the bottom of the painting the inscription reads. « *Ne desperetis vos qui peccare soletis, exemploque meo vos reparate Deo* ».

The painting comes from the Convent of SS. Annunziata in Florence.

2. - PACINO DI BONAGUIDA
The Tree of the Life (panel)

This complex composition is generally agreed to be painted by Pacino di Bonaguida, a Florentine painter working in the first decennia of the 14th century. In the centre of the painting is Christ crucified to the trunk of a tree, from which come out twelve branches with stylised oak leaves and which are supported by exactly forty eight shields (or medallions) with equally as many scenes from the life of Jesus. In

2

3

4

the pointed cusp at the top, are Christ and the Virgin Mary in glory with Angels and Saints; at the foot of the tree are Moses with St. Francis, St. Claire and St. John the Evangelist, and lower down, scenes from the Creation and the Original Sin.

This painting, carried out for the Convent of Clarisse at Monticelli in the first ten years of the XIV century, was brought to the Academy in 1840 after lengthy delays; it is the most provative and adherent interpretation to be seen of the *Lignum Vitae* of St. Bonaventura which was written in 1274.

3. - TADDEO GADDI (known to be around: from 1327 - died 1366 circa) *Panel with the Adoration of the Magi* (panel)

The small painting was part of a series of twentysix painted panels in multifoiled frames which, joined at the two lunettes with the *Ascension* and the *Annunciation,* formed the decoration of the cabinet containing the holy relics in the Sacresty of Santa Croce. They were removed from Santa Croce in 1810 and taken to the Academy in 1814, during which time four of them were given away to private people and are now at the Academy, including the semilunettes; fourteen with *Scenes from the Life of Christ* and ten with *Scenes from the Life of St. Francis.* A reconstruction of the cabinet in Santa Croce with the original arrangement of the panels has been cleverly suggested more recently by Luisa Marcucci.

The attribution of the little stories to Taddeo Gaddi, already suggested by Cavalcaselle, is today universally accepted, and it is agreed that they were done a little after 1330. The student of Giotto shows in his scenes from the Life of Christ, a clear detachment from the master and reveals his interest " in the Sienese artistic atmosphere and his desire to rise up to an antique Gothic tradition rather than Florentine " (Marcucci).

4. - TADDEO GADDI - *Panel with the Stigmata of St. Francis* (panel)

The reference to Giottoesque iconography on Gaddi's part is very evident in the scenes from the life of St. Francis, especially when one makes a comparison between the panels at the Academy and the Giotto frescoes in the Bardi Chapel in Santa Croce which seem to have been the most direct model; as a proof in an also indisputable manner, this scene with the Stigmata of the Saint. One is able to clarify on Gaddi's part in this scene of the Francescan period a personal interpretation of space with an open tendency towards stage design.

5. - TADDEO GADDI - *Lunette with Madonna and Child* (panel)

The origin of this painting is unknown; many scholars, from Sirèn to Procacci, hold that it is by Taddeo, while others, among whom are Gamba and Salmi, consider it the work of a school or workshop; Berenson judges the benedicting Christ and the Prophets in the tympanum of the frame, work of a different artist, which later Longhi (re. L. Marcucci, *The Tuscan paintings of the XIV century* 1965, p. 64) identifies it with Niccolò di Pietro Gerini. This same frame was in fact put together in a later period than the lunette, in the years between 1340 and 1345. Luisa Marcucci considers that the uncertainty of the attribution was due to the bad state of the painting, instead she perceives in this, « undoubtably a kind and way of painting in the style of Gaddi », and a sure spacial arrangement.

5

19

6

6. - GIOVANNI DA MILANO (known to be around: from 134 to 1369) *Pietà* (panel)

This is the only work signed and dated by the great Lombard painter who worked in Florence towards the middle of the XIV century, and there exists a document which proves his presence in this city in 1346; the picture in fact has an inscription under it which reads « *I, Giovanni da Milano, Painted this in 1355* ».

The Pietà of the Academy ranks among the most important and significative works of the Italian painting of fourteenth century, and comes closely in time to the vastest enterprise carried out by the Master; the frescoes of the Rinuccini Chapel in the Sacresty of Santa Croce. The intelligent play of chiaroscuro designed to produce — especially in the outstanding livid figure of the dead Christ — intense emotional effects, the very sensitive vibration of colour, and the robust way in which it is drawn, the imagination and the composition, like the fine and convincing clarity of the invention (one notes the grouping and almost the fusing of the halo around the head of Christ into a single entity) declare that the great height of this work « is a masterpiece of formal scrutiny and of very intense pathos », and these together show the exceptional gift of the artist of the fourteenth century. « The highest point in the maturing and accomplished synthesis among the rigorous and concentrated human penetration of the Florentines and the excitable capillary of Northem sensitivity » (Marcucci). The panel comes from the Convent of St. Girolamo sulla Costa.

7. - ANDREA DI BONAIUTO, called ANDREA DA FIRENZE (known to be from 1343 to 1377) - *Diptych with the Saint Agnes and Domitilla* (panel)

The exhibition in the rooms of the Academy to the public of this precious diptych of the fourteenth century of St. Agnes and St. Domitilla is from quite a recent date (1960). The painting, which came from the Hospital of Santa Maria Nuova and brought to the Gallery in 1900, was in fact left for many years in the storage part of the gallery and only an accurate restoration, which cleaned it of darkened varnish and of heavy retouching, has revealed the brilliant painting quality and brought to light the exquisite en-graved decoration. The recognition of the painter as Andrea di Bonaiuto by Berenson is also recent (1932).

In the diptych of the Academy, the painter, probably a student of Nardo di Cione, is noted most of all for being the author of the famous frescoes in the big Spanish Chapel in Santa Maria Novella. He shows yet again his liking for « elegant effects » and for rich decoration which certainly are not strangers to obvious suggestions of the Sienese school of painting, influences exerted on Andrea by the art of Giovanni da Milano. The work is dated around 1365.

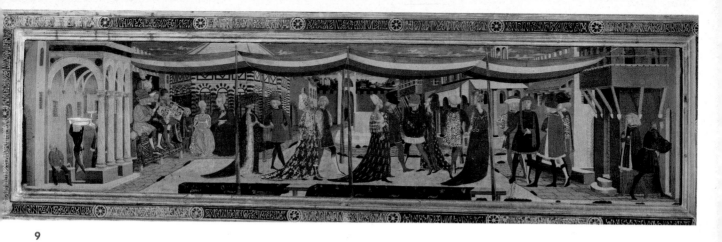

8. - LORENZO MONACO (1370 or 1371-1425?) - *Annunciation and Saints* (altarpiece on wood)

The altarpiece with the Annunciation and at the sides St. Catherine, St. Anthony, St. Proculus an St. Francis, came to the Academy in 1812 from the Florentine Abbey; but one is led to suppose, studying the figure of St. Proculus, that maybe it was originally situated in the tondo of the Eternal cyma in a church dedicated to this Saint, and closed in 1788 (Procacci) and the two angels by different authors. The attribution to Lorenzo Monaco is generally accepted, although the work was for a long time mistakenly accredited to Giotto.

The painting is among the most famous of those of the last of the ascetic Camaldolite miniature painters (born in Siena, but from 1390 was already a novice at the convent of Santa Maria degli Angeli in Florence) the most qualified expounder of the so-called « international Gothic » painting in Florence. Together, the abstract spiritualism of the Angel and the Virgin in the studied parallelism of the diagonal lines, the soft and precious fineness of the colour, the sweeping intellectual drawing of the clothes and drapes certify the convinced mystical vocation and unbroken Gothic disposition of the painter.

THE MASTER OF THE ADIMARI COFFER

9. - *Front of Coffer with a Wedding Scene* (panel)

10. - *Detail of the Wedding Scene*

The wedding scene on the front of this coffer, datable from its style as around the middle of the fifteenth century, is not in any way related, as long tradition would have it, to the wedding of Boccaccio Adimari with Lisa Ricasoli, which took place in 1420. It deals without doubt in a scene which is very festive and gay with a refined manner into which are introduced rich features of « polite » taste reminding one of Uccello and Pisanello; it is also important above all as a document, for the fabulous costumes worn by the figures and for the light and colorful Florentine

« outside » (one notes on the left, a very faithful representation of the Baptistery of San Giovanni).

The attempts of the critics who try to identify the unknown author of this painting are many. Among the most relevant that one remembers, are Berenson, who credits the painting to Francesco d'Antonio, and Pudelko with his idea of the « Master of Fucecchio ». Longhi who reconstructed the personality of the « Master of the Adimari Coffer » proposed in 1940, but with some doubt, a possible identification with Lazzaro Vasari of Arezzo.

11. - SANDRO BOTTICELLI (1445-1510) - *The Madonna of the Sea* (panel)

The small panel with the delicate image of the Virgin and Child raised up over a luminous and dreamy marine background (from which comes its traditional title « The Madonna of the Sea ») comes from the convent of Santa Felicita in Florence. The closeness of the work to the art of Botticelli had been previously pointed by Ulman at the end of the last century when the painting was still in a condition which made it difficult to recognise because of its delicate state; the panel was then attributed again to Botticelli by Gamba, while Van Marle considered it to be by

the so-called « Friend of Sandro »; much later other experts (Boek, Berti and Baldini) suggested changing this to Filippino Lippi. The recent restoration carried out has convinced more than one scholar (Procacci, Salvini) that the painting is definately by Botticelli, being an early work of the artist and which, according to Salvini « the attitude of Verrocchio and the lineal tension of Pollaiuolo are themselves anyway free, in sweet abandon which connects it to the *Spring* ».

Please note that:

The Art Works of the Museum of San Marco described here, appear in the present volume in an order leaving out the chronology of each one, but which follows the normal itinerary of a visit to the museum, firstly the paintings in the Cloister, *in the* Chapter *and the* Hospice, *following with those in the corridors and the cells of the upper floor.*

THE MUSEUM OF SAN MARCO

The Museum of San Marco is situated in one of the most fascinating and illustrious parts of the city. The old Domenican Convent is consecrated in its history of famous names — Cosimo de' Medici, Saint Antonino Pierozzi, and its art by the unforgettable presence of two among the most elect representatives of the first Florentine Renaissance, the architect Michelozzo di Bartolomeo and Blessed Angelico, in real life Guido di Pietro Tosini. In this really unique atmosphere, where history and faith, architecture and painting so admirably « find themselves to be of the same nature, and penetrate still the circulation of a particular spiritual and cultural aura » (Berti), the very high religious and artistic arrival of Fra' Giovanni of Fiesole, the Angelico, led towards his own apex, finding his secure and everlasting destination and ideal home.

At the request of Cosimo and Lorenzo de' Medici, Pope Eugene IV, by his Papal Bull on January 21ˢᵗ 1436, gave the Domenican friars, monks of Fiesole, the Convent and Church of San Marco, and ordered its occupants, the Silvestrini monks to move to the Convent of San Giorgio alla Costa. The Domenicans, whose prior then was Fra' Cipriano da Raggiolo, entered San Marco in the February of the following year. Cosimo's interested sympathy for San Marco and the Domenican monks, showed itself very quickly in a much more concrete form, when he started the restoration work of the old friary, which in a short time, under the direction of Michelozzo, underwent radical and impressive transformation.

The Chronicles *of San Marco (recently translated and published by P. Stefano)* describe minutely the dates and progress of the architectural work, to which it seems Fra' Angelico was given a direct part in collaboration with Michelozzo.

We have reason to believe that the work on the walls of the new Convent was already completed by January 6ᵗʰ 1443, the day of the consecration of the Church of San Marco which was also reconstructed by Michelozzo; all this was according to the wishes of Cosimo il Vecchio and his brother Lorenzo, who as Vasari tells us, had ordered that «the Convent of San Marco was to be reconstructed with much more and all the commodities that the friars could wish for. »

One no longer doubts today that the abstract spiritualism of the place together with the impregnated religiosity of the imposing frescoed decorations by Fra' Angelico must have showed traces of the rigorous moral position of Father Antonino Pierozzi, the new Prior and General Vicar and later the Sainted Bishop of Florence, of whom certainly, precise indications have come of his help in making the Convent function, above all religiously. All over the latter, Michelozzo left vivid signs of his art, showing his own language, however, having taken into account Brunelleschi's shining example, he tends for all that, to put it to one side, reworking with talented forms really of the late Florentine Gothic. The architect could not have found better solutions than those of the faultless staircase which is so full of movement and above all the stupendous Library, *a marvel of spacial equilibrium and perfect and very graceful rythms verifying the masterpiece of fifteenth century architecture.*

It is probable that Fra' Angelico and his collaborators started to paint in San Marco while the Convent was still in the hands of the talented remodelling by Michelozzo (from 1438 onwards) working — as already has been said — in strict collaboration with the architect: so that really one can believe, as Procacci hypothises suggestively, that « as soon as the architect had finished building the walls, at once they laid the colours which came from the brushes of Fra' Angelico onto the wet plaster ». On the walls of the Convent therefore, Fra' Angelico spread out his endless theory of human and heavenly figures under the impulse of an uncorrupted and candid faith, recalling with sensitive melting forms the divine people and pure paradisical spirits suggesting an uninterrupted and friendly conversation; arranging the forms, as Berti cleverly suggested, in the different parts of the Convent in harmony with their own precise religious function, so that the figures were able to accompany the day by day ordinated « moments » of the monks. There is no doubt that for such an important cycle of work (in the Dormitory, on the top floor, there are a good fortythree cells with frescoes), carried out in a relatively restricted space of time (1438/9-1446-7), Fra Angelico had to make use of a consistant group of helpers, among whom the modern critic thinks were well known artists, such as Benozzo Gozzoli, Alesso Baldovinetti, Zanobi Strozzi, Benedetto Bonfigli, etc., or reconstructs the conventional personality (« Master of the Annunciation », « Master of the Nativity », etc.). This participation of help and collaboration is however so certainly dominated by the personality of the Master, and so fully adherent with his ideas and dictation, that one can consider Fra Angelico — apart from a more certain and secure signature — as the only true author of all this particular cycle.

For experts it is still a matter for discussion as to what can be the chronological order of the cycle: namely, whether the frescoed decoration was started on the ground floor or on the upper one, and in in which order. To visitors to the Museum however, the presence of Fra Angelico first makes itself felt in the Cloisters of Saint Antonino (in which lunettes by painters of the sixteenth century like Porcetti, Boschi, Rosselli, etc., illustrate the life of the Saint), and especially in the frescoes of the lunettes above the doors and that with St. Dominic at the foot of the Cross in the great Crucifixion in the Chapter next door. After these follow the frescoes in the cells of the Dormitory on the first floor and along its corridor.

The Convent was closed in 1866; it became a Museum in 1869. In the large room of the Hospice on the ground floor, from 1918-1921 many important paintings on wood panels were collected from different origins, so as to form the biggest and certainly the most fascinating gallery of « monographs » known today. Stupendous illuminated books of the fifteenth century are exhibited for the admiration of the public in the glorious Library designed by Michelozzo, these were illuminated by students of Fra Angelico; while works of later artists (among the first of whom was Fra Bartolomeo) tie up in some way with the story of the Convent and are placed on show on the ground floor where towards the end of the fifteenth century Domenico Ghirlandaio frescoed the large and light « Last Supper » on one of the Refectory walls. The cells, one of which was given to each monk, on the first floor, are everlastingly consecrated to the memory of Saint Anthony, Fra Girolamo Savonarola and Cosimo de' Medici; instead, the great Cloister of San Domenico is dedicated to the memory of a vanished Florence, and in which great numbers of architectural fragments and sculptures, dug up in the demolition of large parts of the old centre of the city in the last century, have been collected here.

GUIDO DI PIETRO TOSINI, called the « BLESSED ANGELICO » (circa 1400-1455)

1. - *St. Dominic at the foot of the Cross* (fresco)

2. - *Detail of St. Dominic*

Here the highest moment in the Life of Christ and the Human Redemption is the necessary introduction to this sacred place, and is put in a prominent position — like an enormous visual opening — in the first *Cloister* of the Convent, and it brings very close the founder Saint of the Order. The fresco was « cut up » however in baroque times and badly placed in the frame in which we see it today. If it is true that Fra Angelico « *never painted a Crucifix which did not wet the cheeks with tears* » as Vasari certifies, it is also true that he was only able to arrange with difficulty in his pictures, an authentic feeling of drama (or « self control », as Berti and Argan suggest, or an effective incapacity to recreate sad situations): nevertheless it seems possible to us to read in this St. Dominic, a more direct participation in the drama, a more intense sadness as from one who represents all humanity and is called to contemplate the tragedy of the Man-God in the final and supreme stage. The crucified Christ instead is already beyond all pain, in a world of higher greatness and has anyway reached serenity; the beautiful face shows above all this infinate reconquered peace; the wounded body, exalted in the new fullness of the coloured light is clearly « spacial » and greatly plastic, also in the strong drawing of the anatomy which reminds one together with the flying ends of the sash of the « cut out » looking crucifix of Lorenzo Monaco. For the finished and mature stylistic value, this fresco is rightly considered as among the late works of the Master in San Marco.

3. - BLESSED ANGELICO - *Crucifixion* (fresco)

In the Chapter, open on the north side of the cloister, Fra Angelico carried out the most extensive and spellbinding composition of the cycle. In the background of this great *Crucifixion,* one can see the preparation, owing to the fact that some colour has fallen away, which comes out a fiery red as in a terrible sunset against the pale blue sky. The fresco is among the most discussed in the philological sense, and there are some experts (for example Muratoff) who think that a large part of it was painted by students after Fra Angelico's departure for Rome. Recent investigations put the date of the fresco from 1441 to 1442; as for the attribution, let us agree with those who say that the main part of the painting was by Angelico, the helpers (among which would have been Benozzo Gozzoli, and the « Master of the Nativity ») would have executed the Prophets in the decorative band, many of the Blessed Domenicans in the shield and probably some other help in the lively composition.

While the figures of the « lamenting » at the foot of the cross relate spacially from the lines of the horizontal and from the luminous band above, one cannot say instead that these people relate one to another; of a spiritual analogous unity each one of the « sorrowing and weeping » as Vasari calls them is different — the attitudes and the manifestations of their painful sentiments make one think that the artist wished rather to represent a sequence of individual « meditations » on the theme of the Crucifixion than a direct and collective participation to the drama. It is probable in fact that religious symbolism would have prevailed decisively on every other descriptive interest.

4

The quality of the figures is generally very high however with some flexion; the most intense of the figures is certainly that of St. Dominic, impressive and powerful, absorbed in a mute and ecstatic contemplation, but very important on moral and formal grounds are St. Lawrence, sealed in the heavy dalmatic, St. Ambrose, the dreaming St. Francis etc. The colour however in the changing and delicate passages is brought to the highest vibration that painting and fresco allow.

Logically, the chief characters in the absolute sense of the drama are the three crucifixes of which the most convincing seems to be « the good thief » in the strong construction of the modelling, and in the glowing and spiritualised head from which effectively seems to spring the certainty of the promised eternal reward given a short time before. A clear spacial sense is made by the converging diagonals of the two crosses on either side of Christ, but the projection and isolation of the three images in a space which belongs to them accentuates the distance of those of the human world placed lower down.

4. - BLESSED ANGELICO - *Meeting of Jesus in pilgrims clothes with two Domenican friars* (fresco)

Only a few critics have laid doubts as to whether the five lunettes situated in different parts of the first cloister, are painted by Angelico or not, the majority are in agreement that they are by him. The lunettes made a part in that level of order evidently which is generally followed functionally by the frescoes in the inside of the Convent; in three of these in fact appear three of the principal Saints of the Order in Domenican habits, and if the lunette as it seems, refers to this same story, they are exactly the Disciples whom the Risen Christ met on the road to Emmeus. In this last scene of Christ as a pilgrim (placed logically at the entrance to the Hospice, which was in point of fact kept for such pilgrims) the poetry nevertheless begs on the programmed assumption that figure of Christ, clothed in light, where there seem to be reminders of a late Gothic type in the style of Masolino, however this contrasts from the strong volumetrical figures and the rich gathering of these same people in the revolving space around to the axis formed by the long staff, and closed from recession in perspective by the outstretched arms and the hands which search and interlace.

5. - BLESSED ANGELICO - *Tabernacle of the Linen Guild* (panel)

6 - 7. - *Detail of the Angel Musicians*

The large panel with the *Madonna and Child* and the relating shutters with *St. Mark and St. Peter, St. John the Baptist and St. John the Evangelist,* was painted by Fra Angelico in 1433-34 for the Linen Guild where the Tabernacle remained until 1777; from there it went to the Uffizi and finally to San Marco. The architecture in marble was from a design by Lorenzo Ghiberti and was carried out by Jacopo di Bartolomeo da Settignano and Simone di Nanni.

This painting is the first among the works surely dated by the Master, and assumes a particular importance and significance in how much it clears the position of the artist in a moment of singular change, that is, there is still a persistence of the persuasive Gothic flattery but at the same time already there are hints of the new art started by Masaccio. If, in fact, the insistence of the ductile lineal marks, the rich taste of the material adorned with arabesques and the measured rythm of the folds and drapes are expressions of an old fashioned language in the Gothic sense (the critics anyhow used to recognise Ghiberti influences in the figures on the shutters), the vigorous placing of the images and their clever modelling, the intense spaciality clearly revealed from their construction and the use of perspective in the three scenes of the predella (*the preaching of St Peter, the Adoration of the Magi and the Martyrdom of St. John the Evangelist*) show already that the painter was strongly interested in the new Renaissance experiences.

The glorious and stupendous colours which clothe the distinct forms make the superb « pictoral » vocation of Fra Angelico clearer, especially in the predella where outstanding brilliance of the enamels and interopposing of the splendid chromatic areas reveal the fervid education of a miniaturist. Along a part of the panel is painted the theory of the very celebrated *Angel Musicians,* the elegant and sweet figures of which, clothed in jewel like colours, were destined to form, almost more than any other, the most popular myth of Fra Angelico.

8. - BLESSED ANGELICO - *Flight into Egypt* (panel)

A little after 1450, Fra Angelico painted the shutters for the silver closet of SS. Annunziata in Florence with the help of students (it seems that among these were Benozzo Gozzoli and Zanobi Strozzi). On these shutters, now divided up, figure thirtyfive small scenes (the « *Mystic Wheel* », *Life of Christ* and the *Judgement of the World*) which represent one of the highest poetical and coloristically most intense moments of the art of the Master, from which comes forth new proof although in « another dimension » of the late maturation of Fra Angelico (Berti); only three scenes (*Wedding at Cana, Baptism and Transfiguration*) are by Alessio Baldovinetti.

Of the little stories by Fra Angelico, one of the most important and perhaps the most lyrical is that of the *Flight into Egypt* rich in starting points, affectionate motifs and tender familiar relations; in that sincere group of the Virgin and her Son, covered by her anxious protecting arms, which proceeds with slow steps on that humble path to safety, in the St. Joseph, taken one would say from living, dressed and packed for the journey who follows, tired and on foot with a strained and preoccupied face. An affable light (« natural » light as used by Masaccio) clothes the figures and the rough and uneven countryside which continues as far as the horizon, which is punctuated by wiry Tuscan cypresses making a gradiation in the clear perspective construction.

5

POSTQVAB CONSVMATI SVNT DIES OCTO VT CIRCVCIDERET PVER VOCATV E NOM EI IHES. LVCE. II. C.

ELONGAVI FVGIENS 7 MANSI INSOLITVDINE. PS. XXXXXV. C

SVRGE ACCIPE PVERVM 7 MATREM EI 7 FVGE INEGIPTVM. MACEI. II. C.

9. - BLESSED ANGELICO - *Christ in the Garden* (panel)

Another of the painted stories of the shutters from SS. Annunziata, in which the naturalist interest of Fra Angelico is made acute direct to a point to become a sharp and almost « scientific » curiosity for every single natural element, so many of which compose the landscape within which the scene unfolds itself. One by one they are described — with a miniaturist's touch and a botanist's detail — the leaves on the bushes and trees, and in the same way the pink and white petals of the almond and peach trees, and the ears and stalks of the grain in the grass of the little field. It is a landscape like that of a hill of Fiesole in springtime, with cypresses and olives gathered together — and an indispensable exotic note — the two fleshy palm trees placed in an axis of the composition. The religiosity of the artist is concentrated on the little figure of the kneeling Christ who is recieving the bitter chalice from the Angel; but other interests are well revealed in the front of the picture, the spacial attention by the short stage, the perspective rigours of the ideal semicircle, the suggestion of the Apostles with the monumental impressive figure of St. Peter solemnly placed with clever foreshortening in the centre of the scene.

10. - BLESSED ANGELICO - *The Altarpiece of San Marco* (panel)

Critics are agreed that this panel was by Fra Angelico; it represents the *Madonna and Son, Angels and Saints* (in the front, the Saints Cosma and Damian on their knees, protectors of the Medici) and placed on the main altar of the Church of San Marco before 1443 — the date of the altar's consecration — and was carried out from 1438 until the date already given. The predella was divided up into several parts which now are exhibited in foreign museums with the exception of two which are still kept in San Marco. The splendid colours of the painting were irreparably darkened and partly destroyed by very bad restoration done some time ago.

A prominent example of a « unitary » altarpiece, this panel represents the middle period of the art of Fra Angelico; he has changed to consider now, with fullness of adherence, the matured experiences of the Renaissance; this can be proved by the rigorous assumption of spacial perspective, by the composition dominated by an equally precise choice of escape lines converging on a centre (the throne of the Virgin) and these lines are balanced by the double row of Saints conceived as an architectural function (human figures placed like columns in the nave of the church). Also the drawing of the carpet is done with the same idea of « indication » in perspective. The development in the horizontal sense of the market garden, thick with trees, closes the scene with measured solemnity, leaving a possibility of catching a glimpse of more wide and open spaces.

Rigours of the geometrical lines and the much worked on plasticity of the figures are not able to mortify the intimate religiosity of the image, neither does the joyous fantasy of the artist who does not abstain from the rich description of the materials, of the drapes and ornaments and of the brilliant festoon of roses.

11. - BLESSED ANGELICO - *Madonna with Infant and Saints* (panel)

The painting, which figures the Virgin and Son, with the Saints Peter the Martyr, Cosma, Damian, John the Evangelist, Lawrence and Francis, came from the Convent of Annalena, now closed down; but stylistic and historical observations lead one to think that perhaps it came from another sacred place before that: the date of its execution is positioned in the decennium between 1430 and '40. The surface of the painting unfortunately is deteriorated; but not to a point to impede seeing it, especially for one who regards the fundemental value of the work.

The Alterpiece of Annalena represents the first example of a fifteenth century « unitary altarpiece » that we know of without the interruption of architectural elements between each figure that is, perhaps rising to a « type » of Masaccioesque intervention, as some scholars hypothesise. The Gothic elements, especially in the decoration of the material etc., are not missed out; but already the light is in a higher and more individual function, and the consciousness of a completely new problem is made clear in the « absolute unity of the altarpiece in a perspective space, concluded with a symbolised architecture ». (Berti)

PARAVERVNT PASCA 7 CVM ESSET HORA DISCVBVIT YHS 7 DVODIM DISCIPVLI. LVCE. XXII. C

NETIMEA QVIA TECV SVM EGO DEVS CONFORTAVI TE. YSAIE. XXXXI. C

APPARVIT AT EI ANGELVS DECEL CONFORTANS EVM. LVCE. XXII. C

FACIEM MAI N AVT ABICREPATIB 7 COSPVETIB IME. ISAIE. V. C

9

11

12. - BLESSED ANGELICO - *Deposition* (panel)

Lorenzo Monaco was commissioned by Palla Strozzi to do the panel for the Sacresty of St. Trinita in Florence, but it was interrupted in 1425 by the death of the artist who was able only to carry out the pointed cusp and the predella (this actually can be found in the Academy Gallery): the intervention by Fra Angelico, and therefore the execution of the altarpiece, is dated by experts as being between 1435 and 1440.

This painting already praised so greatly by Vasari, represents the highest point in the maturity of the Master and for some (Berti) the greatest masterpiece of the artist. The perfect equilibrium of the composition is dominated by the figure of Christ placed daringly on the diagonal, and cleverly accentuated in the group of people opposite, on solidly anchored and very precisely « hinged » perspective (by the two men high on the verticals of the crosses and the ladders and the two Saints on their knees at the bottom); the firm and at the same time graceful placing of the human image, the glory of the colours taken to an unconquerable blaze, the wonderful dosage of light,

crystally and softly broken up and consumed, give the exact measure of Fra Angelico in this very happy moment. Besides these things, another of the fundamental components of the art of Angelico becomes apparent from the panel, interest by now conspicuous, for the landscape conceived is like a « selfgoverning » fact and endows real value and not just an element of support to the background so as to represent action. Here on the right runs the minute and very poetic description of the plain between the rocky or rounded mounts, crowned with castles and houses beaten with radiant light; on the left one sees the stupifying « Jerusalem » with its roads, hedges, ploughed field, trees and haystacks, outside the climbing bends of the walls topped with towers, toward the incongruous mass of the Temple. which is crowded to the sides with squared up and coloured little houses like those in a child's game.

According to tradition, the figure of the bearded man with the black beret on the right of Christ, is a portrait of Michelozzo.

13. - BLESSED ANGELICO - *The Judgement of the World - Detail of the Angels*
14. - *The Judgement of the World - Detail of the Blessed*

The most notable and famous work of the painter Friar. Originally it was in the Camoldese church of Santa Maria degli Angeli in Florence, and previously Vasari described it as « a Paradise and an Inferno of tiny figures: which, with careful observation makes the blessed, very beautiful and full of jubilation and celestial joy; and the damned, prepared for the pains of the Inferno, in various very sorrowful guises and on their alarmed faces wearing their shame and unworthyness »; the panel, as its form clearly indicates, formed the upper part of the chair used by the official during the solemn Mass. The probable date of the work is between 1430 and '33 (a little beforehand according to Salmi), and its authorship seems to be

almost integral, in spite of the contrary opinions of some scholars.

If in the Inferno, rich however with pungent, and very vivid episodes, the artist dwells, as has been noted, on « Gothic spaciality » in his schemes (the interpretation of the place and the pain is still, in fact, mediaeval and « Dantesque »), a lucid and convinced spacial sensibility, understanding in an openly Renaissance sense, is proclaimed instead in the Blessed circle in the splendid garden, in the semicircle of the Saints around the luminous « almond » of Christ, and above all in the dazzling perspective of the wide open tombs. Charming and light « paradisical » images people the wonderful composition, which is rich with precious chromatic and brillant notes.

15. - BLESSED ANGELICO - *Madonna of the Star* (panel)

The tiny and very refined panel (0,84x0,51) metres) is so-called because of the golden star which stands out on the front of the Virgin on her blue cape. The little icon, whose preciosity is made by the combination of the wooden carving and the subtle burination, was in reality a reliquary, carried out with

another three by Fra Angelico for Santa Maria Novella, on a commission given by Fra Giovanni Zanobi Masi (died 1434): two of the reliquaries, those with the *Annunciation and the Adoration of the Magi* and the *Coronation of the Virgin*, are today in San Marco together with this; the fourth tabernacle lost in 1845,

16

was identified with a panel in the Gardner Museum in Boston. *The Madonna of the Star* is dated by scholars in oscillating terms as between 1425 and '34.

Once again it is useful to observe how the painting of Angelico is prevalently displayed — which has value even in this case — in a limpid arch, drawing Gothic suggestions, with motifs and tendenceis derived from the artist's miniaturist experience on one hand; while an always clearer attention to the Renaissance trends is exactly determined on the other hand, as has been attempted in the little panel in the clear foreshortening of the benedicting Christ high up, in the research of an undeniable concreteness in the however always « airy » little figures of the Angels, and above all in the solemn, strong placing of the figure of the Virgin.

16. - BLESSED ANGELICO - *Annunciation* (fresco)
17. - *Detail of the Angel*
18. - *Detail of the Madonna*

The fresco of the Annunciation is purposely placed at the entrance to the Dormitory on the first floor of the convent, as soon as the top of the beautiful Michelozzian staircase is reached, and one can consider this fresco as the necessary introduction to the enchanting sacred stories illustrated on the walls of the cells. The spiritual scene of the « angel greeting », a subject especially dear to the painter, appears the

15

most worthy to represent, in its prechosen place, the guise of a beginning and an invitation to prayer (*Virginis intacte cum veneris ante figuram, pretereundo cave ne sileatur ave,* cautions the inscription below). Though there were doubts formulated by critics, of the overall execution by Angelico of this famous fresco, for which Bazin coined a « Master of the Annunciation », the freshness, the *piety,* the grace and in general the quality of the extraordinary composition are so great as to make one instead convinced, as to his complete authorship (previously Cavalcaselle had seen in this work one of the most perfect creations of the artist).

The scene takes place in a silent portico on Michelozzian lines, facing onto a meadow which has a market garden, thick with moist shadows as its background; the Angel has just appeared on earth and starts to kneel down; the astonished Virgin draws back into herself — the line of her body flexes in measured opposition to the described curve of the agile figure of the messenger. If the space in which the figures are moving is correctly defined as in terms of the fifteenth century, then the personages themselves reflect a sentiment of expressed line in melodic terms which is almost Gothic.

19. - BLESSED ANGELICO - *Noli me tangere* (fresco)

This fresco opens the series of paintings in the cells on the left side starting from the entrance from the second corridor of the *Dormitory,* and mostly by the hand of Angelico. More that one critic confirms that in these frescoes the religiosity of the artist shows itself in a guise made still clearer, and more convincing not found elsewhere while seizing an opportunity which is offered here of a « conversation with each single brother » (Berti), and obeys at the same time, though with some extension of theme, a rule which he wanted in every cell, of « *an image of the Crucifixion, or of the Blessed Virgin or of Sainted*

Father Dominic, the founder ».

Precisely, in the first cell is the poetic meeting between the resurrected Christ and Mary Magdalen in the very green garden (an authentic « Paradise ») thick with our domestic and exotic trees and flowering clumps where Christ wanders about lightly, giving off a whiteness from His clothes and person and Himself lighting up the kneeling Mary Magdalen. The pure range of colours, but moreover a sense of magic, an atmosphere illuminated and suspended, determines the « atmosphere » of almost all of the paintings following this one.

20. - BLESSED ANGELICO - *Deposition in the sepulcre* (fresco)

Attributed by Pope-Hennessy to a « Master of the 2nd cell » and by Bazin to the « Master of the Nativity » (conventional personalities given to non-identified collaborators of Angelico at San Marco), this fresco is instead considered by Berti to be by Fra Angelico, notwithstanding some loss of quality and in spite of the typological diversities noted by scholars (Bellardoni). Undoubtedly, also in this case, as has already been observed, the general idea of the painting and its compositional design, belong to the Master.

The group of personages around the body of Christ is enclosed in a winding oval geometrical form and is made, by the stony spur low down and by the ingenious rocky arcosolium in which one can determine the sarcophagus in very clear perspective. In homage to the already shown didactic necessity of the convent, the emblematic St. Dominic joins with the figures of the protagonists in the act of participant contemplation.

21

21. - BLESSED ANGELICO - *Annunciation* (fresco)

No doubts have been put forward by critics as to the full authorship of this fresco (only Pope-Hennessy had doubts about the figure of S. Peter the Martyr), it is maybe the greatest, and for Salmi, the « most noble » of all in the sequence of cells by Fra Angelico, of which the incorporated and intensely spiritual images have ben pointed out as « the trascendent and no more *representative significance* » (Bellardoni).

In the closed and very pure space marked by the Michelozzian cross-vault, the Angel in his long purple tunic and multicoloured curved wings seems to advance miraculously, hardly touching the ground, aware of his own exceptional mission; the Virgin this time shown kneeling in prayer, seems even more slender and fragile in the mantle which falls swirling in lengthened rythm. To contrast with the luminous celestial beauty of the two figures, St. Peter the Martyr with his cruelly wounded tonsured head appears little less than an intrusion; and his presence, made necessary by the requirements of the Order, breaks the intimate and secret enchantment of the meeting.

22. - SCHOOL OF ANGELICO - *Nativity* (fresco)

This is among the most discussed frescoes of the whole series. Berti recognised the compositional idea as being of the Master (who repeats the same concept in one of the little stories on the shutters from SS. Annunziata) and above all in the very clear perspective placing of the stable; other experts (Francini-Ciaranfi, Salmi) also see some intervention in it by Fra Angelico; Pope-Hennessy attributes it to « the Master of the cell n. 2 », and finally, Bazin, to an equally hypothetical « Master of the Nativity ».

Here also are two Saints extraneous to the real event — the unfailing St. Peter the Martyr and the beautiful St. Catherine who assist the scene in the space in front of the stable, illuminated by the light which comes from the waxen infant, adored by the mother and the plastically painted St. Joseph. These people, arranged apparently without a precise connection, are in fact linked together by escape lines, forming a unique perspective design, which centres on the manger. Angels sing hosannas from the roof of the stable and from the stalls, the ox and the ass lean out curiously.

23. - BLESSED ANGELICO - *Transfiguration* (fresco)

The masterly use of light conducted to identify itself with the same colour for the whole imbibation, so that the images seem to shine with their own luminosity and the grandiose conception make this fresco one of the most high and conspicuous works of Fra Angelico, to whom the picture is unanimously attributed (with one reservation — that of Bazin).

On a spur of the rocky pyramid rises up the immense figure of Christ (maybe the Christ of the Crucifix of Masaccio in Santa Maria Nuova is an ancestor to this?), which gives with its own height and the width of the arms a measure of unlimited space and together the divine embrace turned ideally to all humanity. The religious symbolism is intensified on the heads of the Prophets linked together in the supernatural space revolving around the incandescent oval of the figures of the Virgin and St. Dominic, half divine and half human; a clear separation beteen transcendent and hearth — it is noted — is stabilised by the level of the rock on which stands Christ, and who none of the very beautiful figures of the Apostles, expressed in an extraordinary variety of postures, exell in height.

24. - BLESSED ANGELICO - *Christ mocked* (fresco)

25. - *Detail of St. Dominic*

The representation alluding to the « implements » of the Passion now started, is never more thick with medieval symbolism (the impious and vulgar gesture of the rascal, the hands and the staff raised to persecute) than in this scene of Christ mocked in the praetorium. In it are three of the most splendid figures by Fra Angelico: that of Christ in white clothes, motionless in a painful and patient nobility, with the very beautiful face visible from under the transparent bandage; that of the Virgin, concentrated in a memory of remote and real suffering, the absent gaze with her eyes still showing signs of tears; finally among the most touching and intense of all the painting of Fra Angelico, that of St. Dominic absorbed in profound and moving meditation. The Saint is in the act of preparing to study and meditate so as to complete a high mission; the whole scene besides, with the already noted accentuation of the religious symbolism and the insistent worth of more mediate than direct representation, (the same figure of Christ is as though detached from present reality by the green placard on his back) is to interpret and this is not the only one, like a lesson « per exempla » on sacred texts, and like an invitation to a spiritual concentration on the theme of those proposals. The high and significative mystic abstraction which prevails in the scene has nevertheless not deterred the painter from also considering concrete reality, above all in the sense of spacial representation, in that the images of the three main characters, appear tightly linked together by means of the construction of a pyramid of glowing perspective.

26. - SCHOOL OF ANGELICO - *The Marys at the Sepulcre* (fresco)

Although this scene, in which « notable lacks of balance of style » have been pointed out, is unanimously considered as by the School of Angelico, it is nevertheless interesting to note in it the « lesson » of the Master (from which however one cannot totally exclude his intervention). It is determined above all, towards ends of perspective construction, evidently regulated by the lines of the empty sepulcre, on the edge of which the incredulous Virgin supports herself, shading her eyes with her right hand from the sun so as to see better into the depths.

The « new fourteenth century », which more than once has been mentioned regarding certain later attitudes, so to say, of Fra Angelico, can well be invoked in this fresco for the three feminine figures on the right, models and precedents of which are not difficult to seek and find in Florentine painting from the middle of the fourteenth century onwards. Though remaining a Gothic type atmosphere — but not here downright Gothic — the most lively and singular figure of the scene is that of the rich and elegant Angel sitting on the edge of the sarcophagus, all in white, from the curly and « platinum » hair as far as the little pointed and flashing foot suspended in mid-air.

27. - BLESSED ANGELICO - *Coronation of the Virgin* (fresco)

In spite of the limitations proposed in philological circles by only a few critics (Wurm, Van Marle), there is no doubt that this fresco, as wonderful in its inventions as in its execution, can point competently to the knowledge of an integral autography. The shrewd deducted and spacial arrangement of the saintly figures low down, also participants in this special sort of « grand finale », to the glorification which envelops together earth and sky, the empty atmosphere, which nevertheless detaches with clear illusion to an infinite space, from the ethereal and white mist, from the many coloured contours within which sits the triumphant group of Christ and the Virgin; these give off a personality not otherwise identifiable except as that of the Master.

The faces, the figures mantled in a radiant beauty, signifying a fully reached spiritual perfection; this beauty so great touches a paradisical height in the heavenly and splendid figure of the Virgin; she is typologically like the Annunciation of the 3rd cell, but here she is transfigured by the glorious and supernatural light of the celestial triumph. Connecting the semicircular line of the curvature which closes the top of the fresco with that analogous and contrary description of the Saints lower down, the artist has tried to enclose the whole scene in an ideal group, from which the clear indication « of perfection and fulfilment » already cleverly seen by Berti, does not escape.

28

28. - BLESSED ANGELICO - *Madonna with Infant and Saints*

The date of this fresco carried out on the walls of the second corridor and said to be completely by Angelico, is probably that which was suggested by Salmi, of 1439: at the beginning that is, of the painter's activity in San Marco.

A high poetical intonation, together with limpid compositional coherence and tight formal beauty, characterises this painting, in which eight Saints (from the left: Saints Dominic, Cosma, Damian, Mark, John the Evangelist, Thomas d'Aquino, Lorenzo, and Peter the Martyr) encircle the enthroned Virgin, Fra Angelico bringing forth again the theme of the « unitary alterpiece », keeping for the two groups of personages,

the same function of lively architecture carried out on the panel contemporary with it in San Marco, with profound knowledge of the spacial and perspective data. It is completed with absolute clearness by the illusionistic theme of the pilaster, of the frames, by the same throne in the profound niche within which the spiritual Madonna, who holds the very beautiful Infant from the curly and luminescent head, on her knees, finds her perfect place. A peaceful warm light pervades the scene, investing the pensive Saints from the side, whose plastic corporeal structure does not diminish the intimate and substantial spirituality.

I N D E X

Finito di stampare nel Giugno 1968